We Will Celebrate a Church Wedding

Complete texts of the readings, marriage promises, and general intercessions, with liturgical considerations for planning the wedding ceremony.

George R. Szews

The Liturgical Press   Collegeville, Minnesota

Scripture readings are taken from the LECTIONARY FOR MASS, copyright © 1970 by the Confraternity of Christian Doctrine, Washington, D.C. and are used by license of copyright owner. No part of the LECTIONARY FOR MASS may be reproduced in any form without permission in writing. All rights reserved.

Excerpts from the English translation of the *Rite of Marriage* © 1969, International Committee on English in the Liturgy, Inc. All rights reserved.

Nihil obstat: Rev. Robert C. Harren, J.C.L., *Censor deputatus. Imprimatur:* ✝ George H. Speltz, D.D., Bishop of St. Cloud, January 31, 1983.

Copyright © 1983, The Order of St. Benedict, Inc., Collegeville, Minnesota. All rights reserved.

Printed in the United States of America.

Cover design: Ann Blattner

ISBN 0-8146-1288-1

CONTENTS

Introduction 4
Choosing the Readings 6
   Old Testament 8
   Responsorial Psalm 24
   New Testament 30
   Gospel 50
Choosing the Exchange of Promises 70
Choosing the General Intercessions 73
Liturgical Considerations 79
Liturgy Planning Page 87
The Order of Service 88

INTRODUCTION

The couple who present themselves for Christian marriage come to their wedding day with many high hopes. Life for them is just beginning, the future seems bright, they can overcome anything which they happen to meet along the way. The Christian community also comes to their wedding day with high hopes. We hold that married love shows forth something unique about the God we believe in. The God who calls to us from a far distant future, the God whose love has overcome all obstacles to be near us is made mysteriously and invitingly real in human love. This is something to celebrate. And we do!

We Will Celebrate a Church Wedding is meant to guide you to some of the possible choices you may make and some of the liturgical considerations you should have. It will also assist you in making those choices by reproducing the available options for the readings from Scripture, the exchange of marriage promises, and the general intercessions (sometimes called the "prayers of the faithful").

OPTIONS FOR YOUR SELECTION

In this booklet you will be able to choose the following.

A. Readings from Scripture
1. Old Testament reading (pp. 8–23): *choose one.*
2. Responsorial Psalm (pp. 24–29). In many places the music ministers sing the responsorial psalm. If this is not possible at your wedding liturgy, you may choose one of the responsorial psalms listed and the reader may lead the congregation in the response.
3. New Testament reading (pp. 30–49): *choose one.*
   Alleluia. The alleluia is appropriately always sung, and may be omitted if not sung.
4. Gospel (pp. 50–69): *choose one.*

Introduction / 5

B. **Exchange of Marriage Promises**
In exchanging your marriage promises you may repeat phrase-by-phrase after the priest or deacon, say the promises without repeating after anyone, or respond to the questions put to you by the priest or deacon. Choose one of the options listed on pages 71 and 72.

C. **General Intercessions**
The general intercessions may also be a part of the wedding liturgy. If you choose to have them you may write them yourselves or choose one of the options listed on pages 74 to 78.

The final section of *We Will Celebrate a Church Wedding* contains a listing of several *Liturgical Considerations* (pp. 79–85). You may want to consult these pages before you make a final selection of readings, marriage promises, or intercessions.

The selections which you take from this booklet and any other ideas you may have should be recorded on the LITURGY PLANNING PAGE (pp. 87–88) and discussed with the priest or deacon who will preside at the wedding liturgy. The Liturgy Planning Page may be duplicated so that you may give a copy to the presiding priest or deacon and still keep your own record of the wedding ceremony.

All the possible ways in which you might want to express the love of God which has brought you together are not found in this booklet. The Christian community also has a stake in this celebration. The priest or deacon who will preside at this liturgy will also make choices in the prayers they will use and the words they will speak. You are encouraged to familiarize yourselves with the customs of the parish where the liturgy will take place as well as to consider what unique ways you may wish to celebrate your love. Between the two of us—the community and you, the wedding couple—we will celebrate.

CHOOSING THE READINGS

To find just the right words, to be able to capture a sense, a feeling, a hope, a love with integrity and truth—this is difficult. Most of us rely on words that have already been tried and found memorable. Somehow they speak across generations. Somehow they speak truth. The Scriptures are just such a collection of words, words that live because they do speak truth. It is from the Scriptures that you are first invited to make choices about the wedding liturgy.

This first section of *We Will Celebrate a Church Wedding* contains the suggested scriptural readings for use in the marriage of Christians. All of the readings can be found in the Lectionary (the book containing the appointed readings from Scripture used for proclaiming the Word in Roman Catholic liturgies). In this booklet they appear in the following order: **1. Old Testament** (Hebrew Scriptures), **2. Responsorial Psalm** (you would choose one of these only if the music ministers will not sing the responsorial psalm), **3. New Testament** (the Letters and the Book of Revelation), **4. Gospels** (Matthew, Mark, Luke, and John).

The readings in each category give the lectionary number and the biblical reference by title, chapter, and verse. The translation of the Scriptures from the original languages into English is taken from the NEW AMERICAN BIBLE (NAB) version and is commonly in use in many parishes throughout the United States.

In looking over the suggested options for the readings from Scripture you may notice that not all of them refer directly to marriage. The marriage of Christians does not take place in isolation but in the context of the wider love of God and the Christian community. The reflections which accompany each reading are meant to assist you in choosing readings which reflect your understanding of the love that has brought you together and the faith you witness by celebrating marriage within the Christian community.

Please refer to the previous page or to the person helping you plan your wedding liturgy if you are uncertain as to which choices you should make in this section.

OLD TESTAMENT

Lectionary Number 774-1
Genesis 1.26-28, 31

A reading from the book of Genesis

God said: "Let us make man in our image, after our likeness. Let them have dominion over the fish of the sea, the birds of the air, and the cattle, and over all the wild animals and all the creatures that crawl on the ground."
  God created man in his image;
    in the divine image he created him;
    male and female he created them.
God blessed them, saying: "Be fertile and multiply; fill the earth and subdue it. Have dominion over the fish of the sea, the birds of the air, and all the living things that move on the earth." God looked at everything he had made, and he found it very good.

This is the Word of the Lord.

Male and female he created them.

IN THE BEGINNING, A SENSE THAT IT WAS VERY GOOD. Despite the many ways in which we might look at the world today and find fault, find things gone awry, it is possible that at the heart of our lives we may find something very good. The relationship of a man and a woman has the possibility of reflecting one of the deepest secrets of creation—that in the beginning, in God's eye, people were meant for each other. This relationship, our relationships, can be a mirror of what was meant to be.

Choosing the Readings (Old Testament)

Lectionary Number 774-2
Genesis 2.18-24

A reading from the book of Genesis

The Lord God said: "It is not good for the man to be alone. I will make a suitable partner for him." So the Lord God formed out of the ground various wild animals and various birds of the air, and he brought them to the man to see what he would call them; whatever the man called each of them would be its name. The man gave names to all the cattle, all the birds of the air, and all the wild animals; but none proved to be the suitable partner for the man.

So the Lord God cast a deep sleep on the man, and while he was asleep, he took out one of his ribs and closed up its place with flesh. The Lord God then built up into a woman the rib that he had taken from the man. When he brought her to the man, the man said:

"This one, at last, is bone of my bones
  and flesh of my flesh;
This one shall be called 'woman,'
  for out of 'her man' this one has been taken."

That is why a man leaves his father and mother and clings to his wife, and the two of them become one body.

This is the Word of the Lord.

And they will be two in one flesh.

THIS ONE AT LAST! This one at last! These are the legendary words of the man in the Genesis account of creation as he discovers the woman. At first glance this would appear to be the happy ending to a love story, but we know it is not. The story goes on from here. Finding someone is only the beginning.

The story in Genesis is really quite remarkable. God seems to be correcting creation right from the start. The man was not alone (as the opening monologue might suggest): there was the rest of creation; there was his relationship with God. It was not enough, even by God's reckoning, and so there was the woman. Man and woman were meant for each other; people were meant for each other. Relationships are not a luxury but a necessary part of our wholeness in growing up and growing old.

Lectionary Number 774-3
Genesis 24.48-51, 58-67

A reading from the book of Genesis

The servant of Abraham said to Laban: "I bowed down in worship to the Lord, blessing the Lord, the God of my master Abraham, who had led me on the right road to obtain the daughter of my master's kinsman for his son. If, therefore, you have in mind to show true loyalty to my master, let me know; but if not, let me know that, too. I can then proceed accordingly."

Laban and his household said in reply: "This thing comes from the Lord; we can say nothing to you either for or against it. Here is Rebekah, ready for you; take her with you, that she may become the wife of your master's son, as the Lord has said."

So they called Rebekah and asked her, "Do you wish to go with this man?" She answered, "I do." At this they allowed their sister Rebekah and her nurse to take leave, along with Abraham's servant and his men. Invoking a blessing on Rebekah, they said:

"Sister, may you grow
    into thousands of myriads;
And may your descendants gain possession
    of the gates of their enemies!"

Then Rebekah and her maids started out; they mounted their camels and followed the man. So the servant took Rebekah and went on his way.

Meanwhile Isaac had gone from Beer-lahairoi and was living in the region of the Negeb. One day toward evening he went out . . . in the field, and as he looked around, he noticed that camels were approaching. Rebekah, too, was looking about, and when she saw him, she alighted from her camel and asked the servant, "Who is the man out there, walking through the fields toward us?" "That is my master," replied the servant. Then she covered herself with her veil.

The servant recounted to Isaac all the things he had done. Then Isaac took Rebekah into his tent; he married her, and thus she became his wife. In his love for her Isaac found solace after the death of his mother Sarah.

This is the Word of the Lord.

Isaac loved Rebekah, and so he was consoled for the loss of his mother.

IN THE EVENING SUN WE SOMETIMES WONDER WHAT TOMORROW WILL BRING. There are those rare, golden moments that happen to us, catch us off-guard, when we feel swept up in a whole lifetime of feeling. Images come to us from our childhood, our first love, a great disappointment, the loss of somebody we cared about—and they get all mixed up. We may find ourselves crying and not know why.

At times like these we are present to a whole range of experiences and for the life of us cannot figure out how they are all connected, except that they are connected in us, in our living and loving. There may be no logic behind it except the logic of our choices. The evening sun may bring us to our past but it also has the power to suggest that this day ending is only the prelude to another day. All of us and all that we remember and cannot remember will come to the new day. What will it bring? What choices for love and life will we make? How will tomorrow fulfill yesterday?

14 / Choosing the Readings (Old Testament)

Lectionary Number 774-4
Tobit 7.9-10, 11-15

A reading from the book of Tobit

Tobiah said to Raphael, "Brother Azariah, ask Raguel to let me marry my kinswoman Sarah." Raguel overheard the words; so he said to the boy: "Eat and drink and be merry tonight, for no man is more entitled to marry my daughter Sarah than you, brother. Besides, not even I have the right to give her to anyone but you, because you are my closest relative. But I will explain the situation to you very frankly. She is yours according to the decree of the Book of Moses. Your marriage to her has been decided in heaven! Take your kinswoman; from now on you are her love, and she is your beloved. She is yours today and ever after. And tonight, son, may the Lord of heaven prosper you both. May he grant you mercy and peace." Then Raguel called his daughter Sarah, and she came to him. He took her by the hand and gave her to Tobiah with the words: "Take her according to the law. According to the decree written in the Book of Moses she is your wife. Take her and bring her back safely to your father. And may the God of heaven grant both of you peace and prosperity." He then called her mother and told her to bring a scroll, so that he might draw up a marriage contract stating that he gave Sarah to Tobiah as his wife according to the decree of the Mosaic law. Her mother brought the scroll, and he drew up the contract, to which they affixed their seals.

Afterward they began to eat and drink.

This is the Word of the Lord.

May God join you together and fill you with his blessings.

ARE THERE ANY MORE FLOWERS IN THE WORLD? A small child bending over a daisy for the first time does not really know what the flower is all about. The flower is appealing, it is bright and colorful, it smells good, and it is within reach. Are flowers for picking, for smelling, for touching, or for pulling apart? Are there any more flowers in the world?

For a child the flower appears out of nowhere (adults have a vague notion of "how" flowers come to be but still don't know "why" they exist). Flowers are undisguised blessings and there are many more of them in this world than we could ever count.

Lectionary Number 774-5
Tobit 8.5-7

A reading from the book of Tobit

On the wedding night Sarah got up, and she and Tobiah started to pray and beg that deliverance might be theirs. He began with these words:
"Blessed are you, O God of our fathers;
 praised be your name forever and ever.
Let the heavens and all your creation
 praise you forever.
You made Adam and you gave him his wife Eve
 to be his help and support;
 and from these two the human race descended.
You said, 'It is not good for the man to be alone;
 let us make him a partner like himself.'
Now, Lord, you know that I take this wife of mine
 not because of lust,
 but for a noble purpose.
Call down your mercy on me and on her,
 and allow us to live together to a happy old age."

This is the Word of the Lord.

May God bring us to old age together.

GIVE HIM ETERNAL LIFE, O LORD. Each day an old lady slips into church. Each day her prayer is the same: "Give him eternal life, O Lord." She prays for her husband, dead some time already. She has not forgotten him, nor would she. Like so many people in her generation her spouse has died and she is alone.

They were married many years ago. Their wedding picture is more a likeness of grim determination than spontaneous joy. But, that is the way it was in those days. Her children have hinted that she find another husband. She is not interested. Not because she wouldn't like a little companionship, not because she feels bound to a dead man by words said a long time ago; she simply cannot imagine being married to anyone else. Their relationship was special—and for her, it continues to be special.

Lectionary Number 774-6
Song of Songs 2.8-10, 14, 16; 8.6-7

A reading from the Song of Songs

Hark! my lover—here he comes
  springing across the mountains,
  leaping across the hills.
My lover is like a gazelle
  or a young stag.
Here he stands behind our wall,
  gazing through the windows,
  peering through the lattices.
My lover speaks; he says to me,
  "Arise, my beloved, my beautiful one,
  and come!
"O my dove in the clefts of the rock,
  in the secret recesses of the cliff,
Let me see you,
  let me hear your voice,
For your voice is sweet,
  and you are lovely."

My lover belongs to me and I to him.
[He said to me:]
Set me as a seal on your heart,
  as a seal on your arm;
For stern as death is love,
  relentless as the nether world is devotion;
  its flames are a blazing fire.
Deep waters cannot quench love,
  nor floods sweep it away.

This is the Word of the Lord.

For love is as strong as death.

BETH WAS ORDINARY. She carried herself with the same enthusiasm as most teenagers: which meant that she sometimes bumped into things and other people's feelings. She was confident about life—as confident as any adolescent can be. There were pains and losses and times when "I'll just die if I don't get asked to the dance." Through it all, though, she had that unbounded exuberance which is God's gift to the young. It is also their prelude to intimate love.

At fourteen Beth died of cancer. For her the boundaries of space and time were shattered by the enveloping love of God. Confidence is a matter of the heart, not what life brings a person.

Lectionary Number 774-7
Sirach 26, 1-4, 13-16

A reading from the book of Sirach

Happy the husband of a good wife,
   twice-lengthened are his days;
A worthy wife brings joy to her husband,
   peaceful and full is his life.
A good wife is a generous gift
   bestowed upon him who fears the Lord;
Be he rich or poor, his heart is content,
   and a smile is ever on his face.
A gracious wife delights her husband,
   her thoughtfulness puts flesh on his bones;
A gift from the Lord is her governed speech,
   and her firm virtue is of surpassing worth.
Choicest of blessings is a modest wife,
   priceless her chaste person.
Like the sun rising in the Lord's heavens,
   the beauty of a virtuous wife is the radiance of her home.

This is the Word of the Lord.

Like the sun rising is the beauty of a good wife in a well-kept house.

ONE-SIDED MARRIAGES, LIKE A ONE-SIDED ARGUMENT, leave something to be desired. This reading from the book of Sirach comments only on what the woman might bring to the marriage. Because of our culture and increased sensitivity to the dignity of women, this passage serves to highlight the need for complementarity in marriage. Both the woman and the man bring a variety of gifts to their marital relationship. Whatever these gifts may be, they are given for the good and the happiness of the spouse.

Lectionary Number 774-8
Jeremiah 31.31-32, 33-34

A reading from the book of the prophet Jeremiah

The days are coming, says the Lord, when I will make a new covenant with the house of Israel and the house of Judah. It will not be like the covenant I made with their fathers the day I took them by the hand to lead them forth from the land of Egypt. But this is the covenant which I will make with the house of Israel after those days, says the Lord. I will place my law within them, and write it upon their hearts; I will be their God, and they shall be my people. No longer will they have need to teach their friends and kinsmen how to know the Lord. All, from least to greatest, shall know me, says the Lord.

This is the Word of the Lord.

*I will make a new covenant with the house of Israel
and Judah.*

MOMMY, DADDY, WHERE DID I COME FROM? Sooner or later every parent will have to deal with this question from their children. It may not be phrased in exactly these words but children, at some point in their lives, have a need to know where they came from.

How do you answer such a question? Do you stick to biological facts which are certainly true but not the whole truth? Do you attempt to give the child some context, some history which goes beyond biology?

Where we come from is just as much a part of our identity as what we look like and what job we have. All of us come from some place beyond biology. None of us would want to limit our identity to just the facts. Where I come from and who I am are reflections of the heart. This is how we are really known.

RESPONSORIAL PSALM

Following you will find the complete texts of Responsorial Psalms which may be used in the wedding liturgy. You should choose one of these *only if* your music ministers will not lead the congregation in singing the response.

Lectionary Number 776-1
Psalm 33.12, 18, 20-21, 22

> R. (5) The earth is full of the goodness of the Lord.
> **Happy the nation whose God is the Lord,**
> > **the people he has chosen for his own inheritance.**
>
> **But see, the eyes of the Lord are upon those who fear him,**
> > **upon those who hope for his kindness.**
>
> R. The earth is full of the goodness of the Lord.
> **Our soul waits for the Lord,**
> > **who is our help and our shield,**
>
> **For in him our hearts rejoice;**
> > **in his holy name we trust.**
>
> R. The earth is full of the goodness of the Lord.
> **May your kindness, O Lord, be upon us**
> > **who have put our hope in you.**
>
> R. The earth is full of the goodness of the Lord.

Lectionary Number 776-2
Psalm 34.2-3, 4-5, 6-7, 8-9

R. (2) I will bless the Lord at all times.
I will bless the Lord at all times;
  his praise shall be ever in my mouth.
Let my soul glory in the Lord;
  the lowly will hear me and be glad.
R. I will bless the Lord at all times.
Glorify the Lord with me,
  let us together extol his name.
I sought the Lord, and he answered me
  and delivered me from all my fears.
R. I will bless the Lord at all times.
Look to him that you may be radiant with joy,
  and your faces may not blush with shame.
When the afflicted man called out, the Lord heard,
  and from all his distress he saved him.
R. I will bless the Lord at all times.
The angel of the Lord encamps
  around those who fear him, and delivers them.
Taste and see how good the Lord is;
  happy the man who takes refuge in him.
R. I will bless the Lord at all times.

Lectionary Number 776-3
Psalm 103.1-2, 8, 13, 17-18

R. (8) The Lord is kind and merciful.
Bless the Lord, O my soul;
  and all my being, bless his holy name.
Bless the Lord, O my soul,
  and forget not all his benefits.
R. The Lord is kind and merciful.
Merciful and gracious is the Lord,
  slow to anger and abounding in kindness.
As a father has compassion on his children,
  so the Lord has compassion on those who fear him.
R. The Lord is kind and merciful.
But the kindness of the Lord is from eternity
  to eternity toward those who fear him,
And his justice toward children's children
  among those who keep his covenant.
R. The Lord is kind and merciful.

Lectionary Number 776-4
Psalm 112.1-2, 3-4, 5-7, 7-8, 9

> R. (1) Happy are those who do what the Lord commands.
> **Happy the man who fears the Lord,**
> who greatly delights in his commands.
> **His posterity shall be mighty upon the earth;**
> the upright generation shall be blessed.
> R. Happy are those who do what the Lord commands.
> **Wealth and riches shall be in his house;**
> his generosity shall endure forever.
> **He dawns through the darkness, a light for the upright;**
> he is gracious and merciful and just.
> R. Happy are those who do what the Lord commands.
> **Well for the man who is gracious and lends,**
> who conducts his affairs with justice;
> **He shall never be moved;**
> the just man shall be in everlasting remembrance.
> R. Happy are those who do what the Lord commands.
> **An evil report he shall not fear.**
> His heart is firm, trusting in the Lord.
> **His heart is steadfast; he shall not fear**
> till he looks down upon his foes.
> R. Happy are those who do what the Lord commands.
> **Lavishly he gives to the poor;**
> his generosity shall endure forever;
> his horn shall be exalted in glory.
> R. Happy are those who do what the Lord commands.

Lectionary Number 776-5
Psalm 128.1-2, 3, 4-5

> R. (1) Happy are those who fear the Lord.
> **Happy are you who fear the Lord,**
> **who walk in his ways!**
> **For you shall eat the fruit of your handiwork;**
> **happy shall you be, and favored.**
> R. Happy are those who fear the Lord.
> **Your wife shall be like a fruitful vine**
> **in the recesses of your home;**
> **Your children like olive plants**
> **around your table.**
> R. Happy are those who fear the Lord.
> **Behold, thus is the man blessed**
> **who fears the Lord.**
> **The Lord bless you from Sion:**
> **may you see the prosperity of Jerusalem**
> **all the days of your life.**
> R. Happy are those who fear the Lord.

Lectionary Number 776-6
Psalm 145.8-9, 10, 15, 17-18

> R. (9) The Lord is compassionate to all his creatures.
> **The Lord is gracious and merciful,**
> **slow to anger and of great kindness.**
> **The Lord is good to all**
> **and compassionate toward all his works.**
> R. The Lord is compassionate to all his creatures.
> **Let all your works give you thanks, O Lord,**
> **and let your faithful ones bless you.**
> **The eyes of all look hopefully to you,**
> **and you give them their food in due season.**
> R. The Lord is compassionate to all his creatures.
> **The Lord is just in all his ways**
> **and holy in all his works.**
> **The Lord is near to all who call upon him,**
> **to all who call upon him in truth.**
> R. The Lord is compassionate to all his creatures.

Lectionary Number 776-7
Psalm 148.1-2, 3-4, 9-10, 11-12, 12-14

    R. (12) Let all praise the name of the Lord.
    Praise the Lord from the heavens,
        praise him in the heights;
    Praise him, all you his angels,
        praise him, all you his hosts.
    R. Let all praise the name of the Lord.
    Praise him, sun and moon;
        praise him, all you shining stars.
    Praise him, you highest heavens,
        and you waters above the heavens.
    R. Let all praise the name of the Lord.
    You mountains and all you hills,
        you fruit trees and all you cedars;
    You wild beasts and all tame animals,
        you creeping things and you winged fowl.
    R. Let all praise the name of the Lord.
    Let the kings of the earth and all peoples,
        the princes and all the judges of the earth,
    Young men too, and maidens,
        old men and boys.
    R. Let all praise the name of the Lord.
    Praise the name of the Lord,
        for his name alone is exalted;
    His majesty is above earth and heaven,
        and he has lifted up the horn of his people.
    R. Let all praise the name of the Lord.
    R. Or: Alleluia.

NEW TESTAMENT

Lectionary Number 775-1
Romans 8.31-35, 37-39

A reading from the letter of Paul to the Romans

If God is for us, who can be against us? Is it possible that he who did not spare his own Son but handed him over for the sake of us all will not grant us all things besides? Who shall bring a charge against God's chosen ones? God, who justifies? Who shall condemn them? Christ Jesus, who died or rather was raised up, who is at the right hand of God and who intercedes for us?

Who will separate us from the love of Christ? Trial, or distress, or persecution, or hunger, or nakedness, or danger, or the sword? Yet in all this we are more than conquerors because of him who has loved us. For I am certain that neither death nor life, neither angels nor principalities, neither the present nor the future, nor powers, neither height nor depth nor any other creature, will be able to separate us from the love of God that comes to us in Christ Jesus, our Lord.

This is the Word of the Lord.

Who will separate us from the love of Christ?

WE BEGIN WITH SO MANY HIGH HOPES, promises which we say we'll keep forever, and we look for a place of security to hang those high hopes, some hidden cranny that will hold our promises safely, but underneath it all there may be just the vaguest sense of dis-ease. Can anyone say "for sure"? Can anyone say "forever"? There are all sorts of forces out there, unseen and unbidden. What might they do to a relationship? What might they do to our relationship?

Paul, writing to the church in Rome, has a certain surety about him. He looks at the world with a realistic if not wary eye and affirms: "For sure," "forever," nothing can separate him (and us) from the love of Christ. What a gift! Many people struggle much of their lives for such surety. Paul holds it out as a fact he has come to believe in, and an invitation to believe for the rest of us.

32 / Choosing the Readings (New Testament)

Lectionary Number 775-2
Long Version: Romans 12.1-2, 9-18

A reading from the letter of Paul to the Romans

Brothers, I beg you through the mercy of God to offer your bodies as a living sacrifice holy and acceptable to God, your spiritual worship. Do not conform yourselves to this age but be transformed by the renewal of your mind, so that you may judge what is God's will, what is good, pleasing and perfect.

Your love must be sincere. Detest what is evil, cling to what is good. Love one another with the affection of brothers. Anticipate each other in showing respect. Do not grow slack but be fervent in spirit; he whom you serve is the Lord. Rejoice in hope, be patient under trial, persevere in prayer. Look on the needs of the saints as your own; be generous in offering hospitality. Bless your persecutors; bless and do not curse them. Rejoice with those who rejoice, weep with those who weep. Have the same attitude toward all. Put away ambitious thoughts and associate with those who are lowly. Do not be wise in your own estimation. Never repay injury with injury. See that your conduct is honorable in the eyes of all. If possible, live peaceably with everyone.

This is the Word of the Lord.

Short Version: Romans 12.1-2, 9-13

A reading from the letter of Paul to the Romans.

Brothers, I beg you through the mercy of God to offer your bodies as a living sacrifice holy and acceptable to God, your spiritual worship. Do not conform yourselves to this age but be transformed by the renewal of your mind so that you may judge what is God's will, what is good, pleasing and perfect.

Your love must be sincere. Detest what is evil, cling to what is good. Love one another with the affection of brothers. Anticipate each other in showing respect. Do not grow slack but be fervent in spirit; he whom you serve is the Lord. Rejoice in hope, be patient under trial, persevere in prayer. Look on the needs of the saints as your own; be generous in offering hospitality.

This is the Word of the Lord.

Offer to God your bodies as a living and holy sacrifice, truly pleasing to him.

ONE CAME SEEKING A HEART, ANOTHER WAS LOOKING FOR A BRAIN, THE THIRD WANTED COURAGE, AND THE FOURTH, NOT LIKE THE REST, JUST WANTED TO GO HOME. In *The Wizard of Oz* the Tin Man, the Scarecrow, and the Lion all find something lacking in their lives. They want another chance at life, this time better equipped. Dorothy has left and lost what she had and wants it back. An unhappy beginning to be sure.

All of us want a little more out of life, but is it as easy as the Wizard makes it seem? Can it be done by proclamation? Can we regain what we have lost simply by wanting it more than anything? Paul in this letter to the church in Rome suggests that a transformation is needed. It is not simply a matter of changing your mind, and it can't be done by studying a book. At some point you have to lay your body on the line. You have to act the way you want to become. And maybe that is the secret of *The Wizard of Oz*. The Lion had already displayed his courage, the Tin Man had showed his wits, and the Scarecrow knew he could love if only he had someone to love. Which leaves Dorothy.

Lectionary Number 775-3
I Corinthians 6.13-15, 17-20

A reading from the first letter of Paul to the Corinthians

The body is not for immorality; it is for the Lord, and the Lord is for the body. God, who raised up the Lord, will raise us also by his power. Do you not see that your bodies are members of Christ? But whoever is joined to the Lord becomes one spirit with him. Shun lewd conduct. Every other sin a man commits is outside his body, but the fornicator sins against his own body. You must know that your body is a temple of the Holy Spirit, who is within—the Spirit you have received from God. You are not your own. You have been purchased, and at what a price! So glorify God in your body.

This is the Word of the Lord.

Your body is a temple of the Spirit.

IN OUR COMMON IMAGINATION SEAPORTS ARE NOTED FOR BEING BAWDY PLACES and sailors a rough lot. Corinth was like that. Life was tough and the people there were used to wheeling and dealing—everything was up for sale. In a place where everything has a price tag life can be cheap, priorities for what is important can become flattened.

Paul, writing to the church in Corinth, wants to address this issue but he seems lost for just the right words. He goes round and round the issue trying to remind the small Christian community that they live by a different standard: Christians have an immeasurable worth—really, all people do.

Lectionary Number 775-4
I Corinthians 12.31-13.8

> *A reading from the first letter of Paul to the Corinthians*
>
> Set your hearts on the greater gifts. I will show you the way which surpasses all the others. If I speak with human tongues and angelic as well, but do not have love, I am a noisy gong, a clanging cymbal. If I have the gift of prophecy and, with full knowledge, comprehend all mysteries, if I have faith great enough to move mountains, but have not love, I am nothing. If I give everything I have to feed the poor and hand over my body to be burned, but have not love, I gain nothing.
>
> Love is patient; love is kind. Love is not jealous, it does not put on airs, it is not snobbish. Love is never rude, it is not self-seeking, it is not prone to anger; neither does it brood over injuries. Love does not rejoice in what is wrong but rejoices with the truth. There is no limit to love's forbearance, to its trust, its hope, its power to endure.
>
> Love never fails.
>
> *This is the Word of the Lord.*

If I am without love, it will do me no good whatever.

THE FINAL LIMITATION FOR HUMANS IS NOT DEATH BUT LOVING. We can do all sorts of things that change the way our lives and living appear but we cannot order up love by the next dumbwaiter or bus to Toledo. Love will not come by Greyhound Express. Even if someone were crazy enough to send it that way, we would see right through it.

We humans have an uncanny knack for being able to see through our own actions as well as the actions of others. Though we are not often accused of it, we have an X-ray vision that rivals anything in science fiction. This special vision brings us up against our final limitation: loving. Am I really loving, or am I doing something that looks like loving?

Lectionary Number 775-5
Long Version: Ephesians 5.2, 21-33

A reading from the letter of Paul to the Ephesians

Follow the way of love, even as Christ loved you. He gave himself for us.

Defer to one another out of reverence for Christ.

Wives should be submissive to their husbands as if to the Lord because the husband is head of his wife just as Christ is head of his body the church, as well as its savior. As the church submits to Christ, so wives should submit to their husbands in everything.

Husbands, love your wives, as Christ loved the church. He gave himself up for her to make her holy, purifying her in the bath of water by the power of the word, to present to himself a glorious church, holy and immaculate, without stain or wrinkle or anything of that sort. Husbands should love their wives as they do their own bodies. He who loves his wife loves himself. Observe that no one ever hates his own flesh; no, he nourishes it and takes care of it as Christ cares for the church—for we are members of his body.

"For this reason a man shall leave his father and mother,
  and shall cling to his wife,
  and the two shall be made into one."
This is a great foreshadowing; I mean that it refers to Christ and the church. In any case, each one should love his wife as he loves himself, the wife for her part showing respect for her husband.

This is the Word of the Lord.

Short Version: Ephesians 5.2, 25-32

A reading from the letter of Paul to the Ephesians

Follow the way of love, even as Christ loved you. He gave himself for us.

Husbands, love your wives, as Christ loved the church. He gave himself up for her to make her holy, purifying her in the

bath of water by the power of the word, to present to himself a
glorious church, holy and immaculate, without stain or wrinkle
or anything of that sort. Husbands should love their wives as
they do their own bodies. He who loves his wife loves himself.
Observe that no one ever hates his own flesh; no, he nourishes
it and takes care of it as Christ cares for the church—for we are
members of his body.
"For this reason a man shall leave his father and mother,
 and shall cling to his wife,
 and the two shall be made into one."
This is a great foreshadowing; I mean that it refers to Christ and
the church.

This is the Word of the Lord.

*This mystery has many implications, and I am saying it
applies to Christ and the Church.*

"THINGS AREN'T THE WAY THEY USED TO BE," might be the best slogan to attach to the back of the car in which the bride and groom ride off. It seems obvious, but the obvious is often overlooked.

Too often a couple fall in love, get married, and go on living just as they were before. Nothing has changed. Everything is just the way it used to be except that now there is a piece of paper on file in some county courthouse and some parish rectory. While everyone hopes that through dating and courtship the couple have begun to adjust to a different way of living, it doesn't always happen.

There is no way to insure that a couple know all the implications of marriage. In fact, it might be impossible because the implications will only gradually unfold as the words "for better, for worse; in sickness, in health" come to life. Love, mutual respect, and a realization that "things aren't the way they used to be" seem to be a necessary starting point for marriage.

Lectionary Number 775-6
Colossians 3.12-17

A reading from the letter of Paul to the Colossians

Because you are God's chosen ones, holy and beloved, clothe yourselves with heartfelt mercy, with kindness, humility, meekness, and patience. Bear with one another; forgive whatever grievances you have against one another. Forgive as the Lord has forgiven you. Over all these virtues put on love, which binds the rest together and makes them perfect. Christ's peace must reign in your hearts, since as members of the one body you have been called to that peace. Dedicate yourselves to thankfulness. Let the word of Christ, rich as it is, dwell in you. In wisdom made perfect, instruct and admonish one another. Sing gratefully to God from your hearts in psalms, hymns, and inspired songs. Whatever you do, whether in speech or in action, do it in the name of the Lord Jesus. Give thanks to God the Father through him.

This is the Word of the Lord.

Above all have love, which is the bond of perfection.

WORDS ARE SOMETIMES HELPFUL, AT OTHER TIMES THEY GET IN THE WAY. If you were asked what you think causes the greatest amount of tension in a marriage, what would you answer? In-laws? Money? Children? Intimacy? Religion? Statistics say that any one of these can be an area of disagreement and frustration for the married couple. While any one of these areas might provide the ground for tension, some authorities suggest that the overriding issue is one of communication. Is the couple willing to talk honestly and openly about whatever is at stake? In this case words can be helpful.

There are other times when words can get in the way. Certain words become "red flags" which signal anger and aggression. There are words which indicate only passive agreement, not any real commitment to understand what the spouse is saying. There are words which can make the couple seem far apart and uncaring.

When Paul appeals for mercy, kindness, patience, forgiveness, and gratitude as he does in this letter to the Colossians, he recognizes that for our words to mean anything they have to be supported by an attitude which goes beyond words. There may be times when it is best to stop talking and make way for mercy, kindness, patience, forgiveness, and gratitude.

Lectionary Number 775-7
I Peter 3.1-9

A reading from the first letter of Peter

You married women must obey your husbands, so that any of them who do not believe in the word of the gospel may be won over apart from preaching, through their wives' conduct. They have only to observe the reverent purity of your way of life. The affectation of an elaborate hairdress, the wearing of golden jewelry, or the donning of rich robes is not for you. Your adornment is rather the hidden character of the heart, expressed in the unfading beauty of a calm and gentle disposition. This is precious in God's eyes. The holy women of past ages used to adorn themselves in this way, reliant on God and obedient to their husbands—for example, Sarah, who was subject to Abraham and called him her master. You are her children when you do what is right and let no fears alarm you.

You husbands, too, must show consideration for those who share your lives. Treat women with respect as the weaker sex, heirs just as much as you to the gracious gift of life. If you do so, nothing will keep your prayers from being answered.

In summary, then, all of you should be like-minded, sympathetic, loving toward one another, kindly disposed, and humble. Do not return evil for evil or insult for insult. Return a blessing instead. This you have been called to do, that you may receive a blessing as your inheritance.

This is the Word of the Lord.

You should agree with one another, be sympathetic and love the brothers.

PEOPLE WHO WANT TO MEET YOU HALF-WAY TOO OFTEN THINK THEY ARE ALREADY STANDING ON THE DIVIDING LINE. Any relationship takes a certain amount of balance. When things become lop-sided, out of proportion, or top-heavy, the relationship can break down.

From the perspective of the twentieth-century reader the advice found in the first letter of Peter seems obviously out of proportion. The women in mind seem relegated to an inferior position.

We cannot deny the cultural moorings of the Scriptures. Their concrete life situations in fact give them a validity that is necessary to get at the truth they are speaking. The point of First Peter which goes beyond its time-bound setting seems to be this: the roles and responsibilities in marriage really come from the character of the heart.

Lectionary Number 775-8
I John 3.18-24

A reading from the first letter of John

**Little children,
let us love in deed and in truth,
and not merely talk about it.
This is our way of knowing we are committed to the truth
and are at peace before him
no matter what our consciences may charge us with;
for God is greater than our hearts
and all is known to him.
Beloved,
if our consciences have nothing to charge us with,
we can be sure that God is with us
and that we will receive at his hands
whatever we ask.
Why? Because we are keeping his commandments
and doing what is pleasing in his sight.
His commandment is this:
we are to believe in the name of his Son, Jesus Christ,
and are to love one another as he commanded us.
Those who keep his commandments remain in him
and he in them.
And this is how we know that he remains in us:
from the Spirit that he gave us.**

This is the Word of the Lord.

Our love is to be something real and active.

EVERY MARCH 19TH a well-known restaurant owner in the upper midwest opens her establishment to anyone looking for a meal. Of course this is nothing startling. Serving meals to people who want or need them is what restaurants are for. In this case, however, it is the down-and-out that come in off the streets and are seated at the tables like any paying customer. They will not be charged a cent.

Some people call this a publicity gimmick. Others pass it off by saying that she can afford it now that she has made her money. It is true that she does get a lot of publicity because of it. It is also true that she has made a large amount of money over the years. But this is not the whole truth of the matter. This woman has a deep commitment to the works of justice and charity. March 19th, the Feast of St. Joseph, is a symbol of the life she leads 365 days of the year. The whole truth may not be caught by television cameras or accountants. It will not, however, be missed by God.

Lectionary Number 775-9
I John 4.7-12

A reading from the first letter of John

Beloved,
let us love one another
because love is of God;
everyone who loves is begotten of God
and has knowledge of God.
The man without love has known nothing of God,
for God is love.
God's love was revealed in our midst in this way:
he sent his only Son to the world
that we might have life through him.
Love, then, consists in this:
not that we have loved God,
but that he has loved us
and has sent his Son as an offering for our sins.
Beloved,
if God has loved us so,
we must have the same love for one another.
No one has ever seen God.
Yet if we love one another
God dwells in us,
and his love is brought to perfection in us.

This is the Word of the Lord.

God is love.

WHEN YOU HAVE COME THIS FAR IT IS A GOOD IDEA TO TAKE A LOOK BACK OVER YOUR SHOULDER. There are many things that can be said about God and about humans. When you talk about the two in the same breath the starting point is this: we were made for each other.

The many experiences of love that we have in our lives are all pointers. From the love of parents and friends to the love of our spouse and eventually the love of our children we are directed in a certain way. Not to look ahead, as we might expect, but to look back over our shoulders to the starting point of it all. Love consists in this, that we were first loved by God.

Lectionary Number 775-10
Revelation 19.1, 5-9

A reading from the book of Revelation

I, John, heard what sounded like the loud song of a great assembly in heaven. They were singing:
"Alleluia!
Salvation, glory, and might belong to our God."
A voice coming from the throne cried out: "Praise our God, all you his servants, the small and the great, who revere him!" Then I heard what sounded like the shouts of a great crowd, or the roaring of the deep, or mighty peals of thunder, as they cried:
"Alleluia!
The Lord is king,
 our God, the Almighty!
Let us rejoice and be glad,
 and give him glory!
For this is the wedding day of the Lamb,
 his bride has prepared herself for the wedding.
She has been given a dress to wear
 made of finest linen, brilliant white."
(The linen dress is the virtuous deeds of God's saints.)
The angel then said to me: "Write this down: Happy are they who have been invited to the wedding feast of the Lamb."

This is the Word of the Lord.

Happy are those who are invited to the wedding feast of the Lamb.

B̲ECAUSE YOU HAVE SHARED IN OUR LIVES BY YOUR FRIENDSHIP AND LOVE, WE WISH TO SHARE OUR JOY WITH YOU. WE INVITE YOU. . . . Invitations are a part of weddings. A celebration is not a celebration unless we let other people in on it.

It seems ironic that one of the most intimate things that happens in peoples' lives is not a private affair but something that is recognized and cherished by the entire community. Love is like that, though. Real love, like real joy, cannot be contained or hidden.

GOSPEL

Lectionary Number 778-1
Matthew 5.1-12

✛ *A reading from the holy gospel according to Matthew*

When Jesus saw the crowds he went up on the mountainside. After he had sat down his disciples gathered around him, and he began to teach them:
"How blest are the poor in spirit: the reign of God is theirs.
Blest too are the sorrowing; they shall be consoled.
[Blest are the lowly; they shall inherit the land.]
Blest are they who hunger and thirst for holiness; they shall have their fill.
Blest are they who show mercy; mercy shall be theirs.
Blest are the single-hearted for they shall see God.
Blest too are the peacemakers; they shall be called sons of God.
Blest are those persecuted for holiness' sake; the reign of God is theirs.
Blest are you when they insult you and persecute you and utter every kind of slander against you because of me.
Be glad and rejoice, for your reward in heaven is great."

This is the gospel of the Lord.

Rejoice and be glad, for your reward will be great in heaven.

SOMETIMES OUR BEST INTENTIONS GIVE US THE WORST RESULTS. Sometimes love hurts. It is not always a matter of the way things should be, but rather the way they eventually turn out.

If all of us had our way in the world things would be different. There would be no more hungry, the poor would have enough, peacemakers would have a field day, and the single-hearted would be rewarded. But that is not the way it is. It may not be fair, it may not be the way we would have wanted it, but there are hungry people, there are poor people, and peace seems far off.

When Jesus speaks as he does here in the Beatitudes, he is a realist, but he is more than that—he is also a visionary. Jesus asserts that none of what we call misfortune or injustice, nothing of the way things turn out, is lost on God. More than that, if we could see as God does, as Jesus does, we would also know what really matters. It is always a question of the heart.

Lectionary Number 778-2
Matthew 5.13-16

✢ *A reading from the holy gospel according to Matthew*

Jesus said to his disciples: "You are the salt of the earth. But what if salt goes flat? How can you restore its flavor? Then it is good for nothing but to be thrown out and trampled underfoot.

"You are the light of the world. A city set on a hill cannot be hidden. Men do not light a lamp and then put it under a bushel basket. They set it on a stand where it gives light to all in the house. In the same way, your light must shine before men so that they may see goodness in your acts and give praise to your heavenly Father."

This is the gospel of the Lord.

You are the light of the world.

THERE IS ENOUGH DARKNESS IN THE WORLD, ENOUGH BLANDNESS, TO MAKE US ALL STALE. What we need, desperately need, are a few courageous souls to show us that there is more to life than we are willing to settle for.

54 / Choosing the Readings (Gospel)

Lectionary Number 778-3
Long Version: Matthew 7.21, 24-29

✢ *A reading from the holy gospel according to Matthew*

Jesus said to his disciples: "None of those who cry out, 'Lord, Lord,' will enter the kingdom of God but only the one who does the will of my Father in heaven.

"Anyone who hears my words and puts them into practice is like the wise man who built his house on rock. When the rainy season set in, the torrents came and the winds blew and buffeted his house. It did not collapse; it had been solidly set on rock. Anyone who hears my words but does not put them into practice is like the foolish man who built his house on sandy ground. The rains fell, the torrents came, the winds blew and lashed against his house. It collapsed under all this and was completely ruined."

Jesus finished this discourse and left the crowds spellbound at his teaching. The reason was that he taught with authority and not like the scribes.

This is the gospel of the Lord.

Short Version: Matthew 7.21, 24-25

✢ *A reading from the holy gospel according to Matthew*

Jesus said to his disciples: "None of those who cry out, 'Lord, Lord,' will enter the kingdom of God but only the one who does the will of my Father in heaven.

"Anyone who hears my words and puts them into practice is like the wise man who built his house on rock. When the rainy season set in, the torrents came and the winds blew and buffeted his house. It did not collapse; it had been solidly set on rock."

This is the gospel of the Lord.

He built his house on rock.

KICKING THE TIRES OF A NEW OR USED CAR ON THE SALES LOT is supposed to mean that the potential buyer knows what to look for in an automobile. Occasionally it is a reflex action, a culturally conditioned move that we have picked up by osmosis. We all play the game. Nobody is fooled. But the instinct—that we should know what we are doing when we make a major decision—is right on. We wish that we knew more about what we are getting ourselves into when we do something major in life.

Authorities are supposed to help us avoid pitfalls. They are supposed to help fill in the gaps of our inexperience and partial knowledge. They can point us in the right direction. Ultimately, however, we make the decision. We do what we think is right and best. And we cross our fingers when the first big storm comes along.

Lectionary Number 778-4
Matthew 19.3-6

✣ *A reading from the holy gospel according to Matthew*

Some Pharisees came up to Jesus and said, to test him, "May a man divorce his wife for any reason whatever?" He replied, "Have you not read that at the beginning the Creator made them male and female and declared, 'For this reason a man shall leave his father and mother and cling to his wife, and the two shall become as one'? Thus they are no longer two but one flesh. Therefore, let no man separate what God has joined."

This is the gospel of the Lord.

So then, what God has united, man must not divide.

THE MOST UNCOMFORTABLE PLACE TO BE IS IN THE MIDDLE. We are used to choosing up sides for everything from sandlot baseball to political campaigns. Betting on the horses, the winners of the World Series, or the fastest car are accepted if not universally practiced events in the life of most Americans. We say betting makes the contest more interesting.

Marriage, however, seems to demand a middle ground. There are not sides in a marriage—even though we often divide our churches into the "bride's side" and the "groom's side." Marriage is not a contest—even though the bride and groom often have separate dressing rooms. Marriage is not a betting game—it is interesting enough the way it is. The middle ground in marriage is a difficult place to be precisely because you have to keep reminding yourself that there are no sides to defend against or cheer for.

Choosing the Readings (Gospel)

Lectionary Number 778-5
Matthew 22.35-40

✤ *A reading from the holy gospel according to Matthew*

One of the Pharisees, a lawyer, in an attempt to trip up Jesus, asked him, "Teacher, which commandment of the law is the greatest?" Jesus said to him:
 "'You shall love the Lord your God
 with your whole heart,
 with your whole soul,
 and with all your mind.'
This is the greatest and first commandment. The second is like it:
 'You shall love your neighbor as yourself.'
On these two commandments the whole law is based, and the prophets as well."

This is the gospel of the Lord.

> *This is the greatest and the first commandment. The second is similar to it.*

THE MISSISSIPPI RIVER BLUFFS stand as sentinels over the course of the river. After hundreds of years of erosion these bluffs still rise above the landscape on either side of the river to guide the currents which flow north to south over 2,348 miles. Only as the river reaches its end do the bluffs gradually relinquish their prominence. At journey's end it is the pull of the Atlantic ocean which welcomes and determines the flow of the water.

In the life of Jesus the Two Greatest Commandments rise above all the stories he ever told or were told about him. In healing the sick or comforting the sorrowing or in debating the Pharisees these commandments cast their shadows over the course of events. In the end they relinquish their prominence only as the welcome call of the Father becomes clearer and the embrace of love irresistible.

Lectionary Number 778-6
Mark 10.6-9

✤ *A reading from the holy gospel according to Mark*

Jesus said: "At the beginning of creation God made them male and female; for this reason a man shall leave his father and mother and the two shall become as one. They are no longer two but one flesh. Therefore let no man separate what God has joined."

This is the gospel of the Lord.

They are no longer two, therefore, but one body.

SUMMARY STATEMENTS CAN BE DECEIVING. They seem so clear and pointed we may think we understand all that went before them and all that is implied because of them when we really do not. To leave your parents, to find a new identity with someone else, summarizes an entire process of leave-taking and loving. You cannot come to the summary without going through the process.

Lectionary Number 778-7
John 2.1-11

✢ *A reading from the holy gospel according to John*

There was a wedding at Cana in Galilee, and the mother of Jesus was there. Jesus and his disciples had likewise been invited to the celebration. At a certain point the wine ran out, and Jesus' mother told him, "They have no more wine." Jesus replied, "Woman, how does this concern of yours involve me? My hour has not yet come." His mother instructed those waiting on table, "Do whatever he tells you." As prescribed for Jewish ceremonial washings, there were at hand six stone water jars, each one holding fifteen to twenty-five gallons. "Fill those jars with water," Jesus ordered, at which they filled them to the brim. "Now," he said, "draw some out and take it to the waiter in charge." They did as he instructed them. The waiter in charge tasted the water made wine, without knowing where it had come from; only the waiters knew, since they had drawn the water. Then the waiter in charge called the groom over and remarked to him: "People usually serve the choice wine first; then when the guests have been drinking a while, a lesser vintage. What you have done is keep the choice wine until now." Jesus performed this first of his signs at Cana in Galilee. Thus did he reveal his glory, and his disciples believed in him.

This is the gospel of the Lord.

This was the first of the signs given by Jesus; it was given at Cana in Galilee.

MIRACLES STILL DO HAPPEN. Or do they? We have become quite sophisticated in our expectations these days. Round trips into outer space, artificial organs implanted in human bodies, test-tube babies all combine to imply that what used to be unusual is now usual. The trend will probably continue as our energies and intellects are applied to what are now only possibilities.

Christians do not hold that miracles are things that happen outside the realm of possibility. Miracles are events in which we see the presence of God in a clear and decisive way. The love of a particular man and a particular woman out of all the possible combinations of men and women in the world can be a miracle if we can recognize the presence of Christ in their relationship.

Lectionary Number 778-8
John 15.9-12

✢ *A reading from the holy gospel according to John*

Jesus said to his disciples:
  "As the Father has loved me,
so I have loved you.
Live on in my love.
You will live in my love
if you keep my commandments,
even as I have kept my Father's
  commandments,
and live in his love.
All this I tell you
that my joy may be yours
and your joy may be complete.
This is my commandment:
love one another
as I have loved you."

This is the gospel of the Lord.

Remain in my love.

How DO THEY DO IT? Have you ever wondered how a man and a woman have maintained a loving relationship over a number of years? Have you ever been tempted to go up to such a couple and say: "How do you do it? Tell my your secret." We all want that kind of relationship: love which withstands the forces that might pull two people apart.

If we ever did ask a couple what their secret was for a long and happy married life we might get an answer like, "Never go to bed angry," or "Make sure there is some time in every day for just the two of you." But these are not secrets, just common sense.

When Jesus speaks in the Gospel of John, the secret of loving is an open secret. Like common sense, it is available to everyone.

66 / Choosing the Readings (Gospel)

Lectionary Number 778-9
John 15.12-16

✛ *A reading from the holy gospel according to John*

Jesus said to his disciples:
"This is my commandment:
love one another
as I have loved you.
There is no greater love than this:
to lay down one's life for one's friends.
You are my friends
if you do what I command you.
I no longer speak of you as slaves,
for a slave does not know what his master is
   about.
Instead, I call you friends,
since I have made known to you all that I
   heard from my Father.
It was not you who chose me,
it was I who chose you
to go forth and bear fruit.
Your fruit must endure,
so that all you ask the Father in my name
he will give you."

This is the gospel of the Lord.

This is my commandment: love one another.

THE NOTE SAID: "I LOVE YOU." The kitchen table was littered with the morning newspaper, an empty coffee cup, two or three coupons no longer redeemable, and a note. It was written on a piece of paper torn from a magazine. The white space in an advertisement for the newest soap on the market carried this penciled-in message: "I love you." There was no signature; none was needed. The handwriting, illegible as always, was familiar.

In a world filled with options from which we are used to choosing, it is good to be reminded that we are the chosen.

Choosing the Readings (Gospel)

Lectionary Number 778-10
Long Version: John 17.20-26

✣ *A reading from the holy gospel according to John*

Jesus looked up to heaven and prayed:
"Holy Father,
I do not pray for my disciples alone.
I pray also for those who will believe in me through
 their word,
that all may be one
as you, Father, are in me, and I in you;
I pray that they may be [one] in us,
that the world may believe that you sent me.
I have given them the glory you gave me
that they may be one, as we are one—
I living in them, you living in me—
that their unity may be complete.
So shall the world know that you sent me,
and that you loved them as you loved me.
Father,
all those you gave me
I would have in my company
where I am,
to see this glory of mine
which is your gift to me,
because of the love you bore me before the world
 began.
Just Father,
the world has not known you,
but I have known you;
and these men have known that you sent me.
To them I have revealed your name,
and I will continue to reveal it
so that your love for me may live in them,
and I may live in them."

This is the gospel of the Lord.

Short Version: John 17.20-23

✝ *A reading from the holy gospel according to John*

**Jesus looked up to heaven and prayed:
"Holy Father,
I do not pray for my disciples alone.
I pray also for those who will believe in me
   through their word,
that all may be one
as you, Father, are in me, and I in you;
I pray that they may be [one] in us,
that the world may believe that you sent me.
I have given them the glory you gave me
that they may be one, as we are one—
I living in them, you living in me—
that their unity may be complete.
So shall the world know that you sent me,
and that you loved them as you loved me."**

This is the gospel of the Lord.

May they be completely one.

WE HAVE CRUCIFIXES AND STATUES TO REMIND US OF JESUS, BUT WHERE DO WE SEE HIM? The memory of Jesus has endured 2,000 years. In that time the recollection of him has been sparked by the stories told about him, the images that have been constructed around these stories, and, perhaps most of all, by the people who choose to be committed to him.

Crosses and statues serve to remind us of Jesus. If, however, we want to see him, we have to look to the lives of his followers. The burden of proof for his continuing presence with and to his people is found in the love and unity of Christians. Just as Jesus was the human face of the Father, so we have become the image of Jesus.

CHOOSING THE EXCHANGE OF PROMISES

The exchange of promises is the primary symbol of the wedding liturgy. In these promises the man and woman call upon the Christian community to witness their mutual consent, their promise of fidelity, and their pledge that the union they enter will be kept for the rest of their lives. Since this is the core of the liturgy, the couple should take care in choosing from among the available options the one which best expresses their commitment. The couple should also take care that the Christian community which they call upon to witness their commitment can in fact hear the exchange of promises.

You will want to choose *one* of the options listed on the following two pages numbered 25.a, 25.b, 25.c, 25.d. For options 25.a and 25.c the couple should indicate whether they will recite from memory (or read off a small card) their exchange of promises or whether they will repeat after the priest or deacon.

THE MARRIAGE PROMISES

Option 25.a

The bridegroom says:
~~I, N., take you, N., to be my wife.~~ *I promise to be true to you in good times and in bad, in sickness and in health. I will love you and honor you all the days of my life.*

The bride says:
~~I, N., take you, N., to be my husband.~~ *I promise to be true to you in good times and in bad, in sickness and in health. I will love you and honor you all the days of my life.*

(The couple may recite these promises or may repeat them after the priest or deacon.)

Option 25.b

The priest or deacon questions first the bridegroom and then the bride with the following words. Each responds, "I do."

N., do you take N. to be your wife? Do you promise to be true to her in good times and in bad, in sickness and in health, to love her and honor her all the days of your life?
The bridegroom: **I do.**

N., do you take N. to be your husband? Do you promise to be true to him in good times and in bad, in sickness and in health, to love him and honor him all the days of your life?
The bride: **I do.**

Option 25.c

The bridegroom says:
I, N., take you, N., for my lawful wife, to have and to hold, from this day forward, ~~for better, for worse, for richer, for poorer, in sickness and in health, until death do us part.~~

The bride says:
I, N., take you, N., for my lawful husband, to have and to hold, from this day forward, ~~for better, for worse, for richer, for poorer, in sickness and in health, until death do us part.~~

(The couple may recite these promises or may repeat them after the priest or deacon.)

Option 25.d

The priest or deacon questions first the bridegroom and then the bride with the following words. Each responds, "I do."

N., do you take N. for your lawful wife, to have and to hold, from this day forward, for better, for worse, for richer, for poorer, in sickness and in health, until death do you part?
The bridegroom: **I do.**

N., do you take N. for your lawful husband, to have and to hold, from this day forward, for better, for worse, for richer, for poorer, in sickness and in health, until death do you part?
The bride: **I do.**

CHOOSING THE GENERAL INTERCESSIONS

The general intercessions (prayers of the faithful) are prayer intentions which reflect the needs of the Christian community as a whole, the world and society in which we live, and the particular community that gathers. As such these prayers should include a broad range of needs. Too often they are restricted to the needs and intentions of the marriage couple. While it is certainly good that the couple want to place their trust in God through these intentions, it is also important that there be a recognition of the wider community which witnesses and celebrates the love of the marriage couple.

On the following pages are three examples of general intercessions. The first is taken from the Sacramentary (the book containing the official prayers of the church used by the priest), and the other two have been composed by the author. The couple may choose any *one* of these samples or compose their own. If the wedding couple write their own general intercessions, a copy should be given to the priest or deacon who will preside at the wedding liturgy and to the reader who will lead the congregation in these prayers.

Option A (Sacramentary: No. 10. ORDINARY TIME II)

Introduction by the priest or deacon:

> My brothers and sisters,
> we are gathered to celebrate the mystery
> of our salvation in Jesus Christ.
> Let us ask God our Father
> to open for all the world this fountain of life and
>   blessing.

Intercessions led by another minister:

A. **For all who have dedicated themselves to God,
that he will help them to be faithful to their promise,
we pray to the Lord:**

   R. Lord, hear our prayer.

B. **For peace among nations,
that God may rid the world of violence,
and let us serve him in freedom,
we pray to the Lord:**

   R. Lord, hear our prayer.

C. **For the aged who suffer from loneliness and infirmity,
that we will sustain them by our love,
we pray to the Lord:**

   R. Lord, hear our prayer.

D. **For all of us gathered here,
that God will teach us to use wisely
the good things he has given us,
that they will lead us closer to him
and to the eternal blessings he promises,
we pray to the Lord:**

   R. Lord, hear our prayer.

Concluding prayer by the priest or deacon:

> Father,
> hear the prayers of your people.
> Give us what you have inspired us
>   to ask you for in faith.
> We ask this through Christ our Lord.
> R. Amen.

Option B

Introduction by the priest or deacon:

> My friends,
> we have come together in the name of the Lord.
> Now let us turn to him and ask him to be near
>   to those for whom we pray.

Intercessions led by another minister:

A. **For the community of believers,
for all who in the name of the Lord fall
    and cannot carry on,
we pray to the Lord:**

R. **Lord, hear our prayer.**

B. **For the people who belong to us,
for parents and friends,
for companions along the way,
for those who have made this day possible,
we pray to the Lord:**

R. **Lord, hear our prayer.**

C. **For justice and rights and loyalty,
that they may be stronger than injustice and
    destruction,
we pray to the Lord:**

R. **Lord, hear our prayer.**

D. For those who live in the shadows
or on the fringes,
for those who are never noticed,
for the ordinary and likeable,
we pray to the Lord:

R. Lord, hear our prayer.

E. For all of us gathered here,
for N. and N. who have pledged themselves
to each other,
that love will not fail us
and peace will come and find a home,
we pray to the Lord:

R. Lord, hear our prayer.

Concluding prayer by the priest or deacon:

Father,
you have bound yourself to us.
We ask you to let us experience your faithfulness
in good and bad times.
Give us what we ask for and what we need.
We ask this through Jesus Christ our Lord.

R. Amen.

Option C

Introduction by the priest or deacon:

Friends,
we have come here in faith.
The memory of Jesus, his deeds and destiny,
call us to place our trust in our Father in heaven.
Let us pray that the Father will hear our need
and take it to heart.

Choosing the General Intercessions / 77

Intercessions led by another minister:

A. For the church,
for all who seek the face of God,
for all who call upon the name of Jesus
for all who rely on the fellowship of the Spirit,
that we will not be disappointed,
we pray to the Lord:

R. Lord, hear our prayer.

B. For our world,
for men and women who bear
    the responsibility of leadership,
for those who provide daily services,
that integrity and justice and compassion
    will prevail,
we pray to the Lord:

R. Lord, hear our prayer.

C. For families,
for those who teach us what it means
    to love,
for those torn and divided,
that love will never be far off
    and peace will find a home,
we pray to the Lord:

R. Lord, hear our prayer.

D. For N. and N.
with whom we celebrate today,
for all of us who have come to be with them,
    and those who could not be here,
we pray to the Lord:

R. Lord, hear our prayer.

> E. For the dead,
> for our ancestors who have kept faith and love alive in this world,
> for those who teach us what it means to believe,
> we pray to the Lord:
>
> R. Lord, hear our prayer.

Concluding prayer by the priest or deacon:

> Father,
> teach us that all passes in this world,
> all except love, the love which you have shown us in your Son Jesus.
> We ask this through Jesus Christ our Lord.
>
> R. Amen.

Option D

You may choose to compose your own general intercessions for the wedding liturgy. If you do, you should follow the example of the sample intercessions in options A, B, and C. Please keep in mind that your intentions should extend to the wider concerns of the Church as a whole and the world in which we live as well as the particular needs that you have on the wedding day.

A copy of your intentions should be given to the priest or deacon who will preside at the liturgy as well as to the minister who will lead the congregation in this prayer.

LITURGICAL CONSIDERATIONS

When a couple present themselves for Christian marriage they are filled with many thoughts and memories of committed love. It is a time like no other for them and they want to celebrate their love in a way that gives expression and meaning to all they are thinking and feeling. The Christian community also comes to the wedding day with many thoughts and expectations. Sometimes all this is confusing. To find just the right words, to think of and include all the important people, to celebrate love and commitment with integrity and faith—this takes thought and preparation.

It is not strange, then, that the Church urges the couple to carefully assist in planning the wedding liturgy. Primarily this will be a time of prayer, one moment in a day filled with other times for socializing and receiving the good wishes of friends and relatives. As you review the possibilities for planning the wedding liturgy you may want to keep in mind the considerations which follow. These principles should help you construct a liturgy which is both prayerful and meaningful.

WHO?

There are many people who are important to you as you come to your celebration of marriage. There are individuals that you will want to have a special place in the liturgy. In the wedding liturgy there is room and even need for a variety of ministers—people who serve the needs of the community that gathers for worship. Here are some of the ministerial roles which you should consider in developing the wedding liturgy.

1. **The Assembly**

    The assembly of believers are all those who will come together with you to witness and celebrate your love and commitment. They are not just observers but people who want to be there to pray with and for you. They celebrate in word, song, and gesture.

2. **Bride and Groom**

    You are *the* ministers of Christian marriage. In a very real sense you "marry" each other in the presence of the assembly.

3. **The Presider**

    The priest or deacon will preside at the wedding liturgy. This means that the priest or deacon has been recognized by the Christian community as a person of prayer and faith competent to lead the community in worship. The priest or deacon addresses the Father in prayer, coordinates the various ministers, and calls the assembly to prayer.

4. **Reader(s)**

    A reader has a distinct ministerial function: to proclaim the Word of God. He or she does this by reading the first and second reading. The reader may also lead the responsorial psalm (if it is not sung) and the general intercessions. There may be more than one reader. In order to fulfill this important role the person you select should be qualified, that is, be able to proclaim the Word of God with dignity and faith.

5. Communion Distributor(s)

If you have a large gathering, or if it is the custom in your parish to distribute communion under both forms, you may, with the help of the priest or deacon, want to choose extraordinary communion distributors.

6. Music Ministers

There may be a number of music ministers:
a. accompanists
b. soloists
c. leaders of congregational song

Since music is an integral part of any liturgy, only qualified liturgical musicians should be asked to do this service. Their ministry consists in proclaiming our faith in song and in helping the assembly pray more deeply.

7. Servers

These "helpers" provide a variety of services. They assist the presider, prepare the gifts, and help in many other ways according to the customs of your parish.

8. Attendants

These people assist the bride and groom. They do this by standing as witnesses and fulfilling other functions which the bride and groom may ask them to do.

9. Ushers

Ushers greet people at the door and welcome them to the celebration. They help the assembly get seated, hand out participation aids when necessary, and assist the assembly wherever they can.

SONG AND SYMBOL

In looking at unique ways to express their love and commitment in faith, a wedding couple often looks first to music and symbols. This seems entirely natural. We are surrounded with music. We grow up learning about life and love listening to songs which express, in memorable ways, what is going on with us and in us. Symbols often express what we cannot find the words to say. Symbols go beyond words, inviting us to new insights and deeper levels of living.

In choosing music for the wedding liturgy the key word is "prayer." Does the music, whether it is instrumental or song, help you and the entire assembly pray? There will be other occasions on your wedding day to listen to a favorite song which is somehow connected to your love. At the wedding liturgy the important question is how the music you choose will help everyone pray. In many parishes the music to be used at a wedding liturgy must first be approved by someone on the parish staff. You might want to check if this is the policy in the community which will celebrate your wedding liturgy.

In looking at symbols or symbolic actions for the wedding liturgy it is good to remember that the primary symbol is found in the exchange of the marriage promises. If these are done clearly, in the sight of everyone present, and if everyone can hear the commitment you make to each other, you have already grounded the liturgy in the best symbol. The exchange of rings is a secondary symbol of the wedding liturgy and may even be omitted. Other symbols or actions which you might want to include should be considered carefully. While the lighting of a unity candle is beautiful, or the presenting of flowers to parents is touching, these sorts of actions should not overshadow or seem more important than the exchange of wedding promises.

WHAT?

What exact shape the wedding liturgy will take depends a great deal on local customs and your planning with the priest or deacon. Generally all wedding liturgies will have most or all of the following parts. (In a wedding liturgy which will not include the Eucharist, however, only numbers 1, 2, 3, 4, 5, and 9 will be part of the service.)

1. Entrance

Since most weddings take place in churches there is a period of gathering, of coming to and entering into prayer. Ushers greet guests and help them find seats. The wedding party forms a procession of formal entrance. It is important to remember that the formal entrance of the wedding liturgy helps people focus their attention on the unique reason for this celebration. An entrance procession which contains just the bride and bridesmaids suggests that only the bride is important. Such a singular entrance does not speak very well of the union of two people. The entrance procession is a good place to include all the ministers of the liturgy as well as the parents of both bride and groom.

2. Introductory Rites

When all have gathered for the liturgy the priest or deacon who is presiding will call the assembly to prayer. Here as throughout the liturgy the presider will choose among various options which are intended to be made by the presiding minister. In some cases the priest or deacon who is assisting you in planning the wedding liturgy will discuss these options with you. In any case he will make selections based on his working with you to prepare for your marriage.

This part of the liturgy will conclude with the presider addressing the Father of Jesus in prayer.

3. Liturgy of the Word

Here the reader(s) will proclaim the Word of God, the priest or deacon will proclaim the gospel and preach the homily and the actual rite of marriage will take place.

Earlier in this booklet you have been given the options for the readings which will be proclaimed during this part of the liturgy. The person who presides at the liturgy may want to discuss with you why you have selected the readings you indicated on the LITURGY PLANNING PAGE. Often this discussion will form the basis of his homily.

4. The Marriage Rite

Within the context of the Liturgy of the Word the sacrament of marriage takes place. The presider will call the community to their role as witnesses and instruct you, the wedding couple, one final time on the duties of marriage. He will then invite you to exchange your marriage promises.

84 / *Liturgical Considerations*

The options available to you for the exchange of promises are found on pages 71 and 72 of this booklet. In choosing one of these options please be sure to specify whether you will recite the promises or repeat after the priest or deacon.

At this time you may also want to exchange rings as a tangible sign of your commitment. If you choose to do so, the presider will first bless the rings and then you will give them to each other with these words: "N., take this ring as a sign of my love and fidelity. In the name of the Father, and of the Son, and of the Holy Spirit."

5. **General Intercessions**

After the exchange of promises the prayers of the faithful are led by one of the assisting ministers. You will find the options for general intercessions on pages 73 to 78 of this booklet. If this liturgy does not include Eucharist the nuptial blessing and dismissal rite would immediately follow. If this liturgy does include Eucharist the preparation of gifts would follow.

6. **Preparation of Gifts**

This is a transition time in the wedding liturgy. The focus shifts from the Liturgy of the Word to the Liturgy of the Table.

7. **Eucharistic Prayer**

The priest will choose an appropriate Eucharistic Prayer and lead the congregation in addressing the Father, praising him for his goodness, and remembering the death and resurrection of the Lord Jesus.

8. **The Communion Rite**

After the conclusion of the Eucharistic Prayer the Our Father begins the communion rite. There is the sign of peace, the breaking of the blessed bread, the call to communion, the distribution of communion and finally the prayer after communion. During this time the priest may also pray a special blessing known as the nuptial blessing over the married couple.

9. Dismissal Rites

At this time the presider will call the assembly to pray for God's blessing and dismiss the gathering. There will then be a recessional of all those who formed the entrance procession.

LITURGY PLANNING PAGE

for the marriage of

_____ and _____

Date of Rehearsal   Date of Wedding

Time _____   Time _____

Presider _____

Attendants

_____ and _____

_____ and _____

_____ and _____

Reader(s)   Communion Distributor(s)

Servers   Ushers

Music Ministers

Music Selections

The Liturgical Press grants permission to duplicate this Liturgy Planning Page.

THE ORDER OF SERVICE

Entrance (any special instructions)

Introductory Rites

Liturgy of the Word (see pages 6 to 69)

    First Reading: Lectionary Number_____

        Title, chapter, verse_____

    Responsorial Psalm: Sung_____ Recited (Lectionary Number)_____

    Second Reading: Lectionary Number_____

        Title, chapter, verse_____

    Alleluia (may be omitted if not sung): yes_____ no_____

    Gospel: Lectionary Number_____

        Title, chapter, verse_____

Marriage Rite (see pages 70 to 72)

    Exchange of Promises: 25.a_____ 25.b_____ 25.c_____ 25.d_____

        Recited_____ Repeated after_____

    Exchange of Rings: yes_____ no_____

    Other instructions for the marriage rite:

General Intercessions (see pages 73 to 78)

    A._____ B._____ C._____ D. Written by couple (please attach)_____

Preparation of Gifts

Eucharistic Prayer

Communion Rite

Dismissal Rite

Special instructions or notations